Yesterday, Today, and . . .

Yesterday, Today, and . . .

Jack D. Goldberg

American Literary Press, Inc.
Five Star Special Edition
Baltimore, Maryland

This collection of poetry is dedicated to my wife, Shirley. In spite of her debilitating illness; it was her inspiration to me to continue to compose poetry which I had set aside many years ago.

A great thanks to Jeffrey L. Cummings, MD, Professor of Psychiatry and Biobehavioral Sciences and Director of UCLA Alzheimer's Disease Center at the UCLA School of Medicine, for giving me a clear understanding of the short and long term effects of Alzheimer's Disease, the dreaded scourge of the elderly.

A special thanks to Wendy Gurga for her keen deciphering of my written words into legible typewritten poetry.

Contents

THE BEAUTY OF THE NIGHT

As darkness covers the earth all is quiet and still.
The din and the bustle of the day is muted if not gone.
The nocturnal creatures of the night pursue their quest for food
and sustenance stealthily along the sewers and gutters of the
sleeping city.
The lights that are ever present are dimmed, by the faint wisps
of fog slowly drifting in from the sea.
The rotating light of the lighthouse, far off in the distance, is a
beacon of hope for those at sea and those ashore.
The harbor lights are shaded and lowered for their need is
lowered in the still of the night.
The bobbing lights of the myriad beats docked and secured in
their slips are as gentle as a rocking cradle.
Too soon the quiet and the beauty of the night will be stolen
away as the world awakens to the activities of the day.
Do not despair, for the quiet and beauty of the night shall return
as the sun sets and the activities of the day are put to rest.
The quiet beauty of the night will once again return as a soothing
balm for our distraught spirit.
Once again all is quiet and still.

ON LOOKING FORWARD

Look forward; do not look back.
Look forward to days of bright sunshine and cooling breezes.
Look forward to a life of joy and happiness.
Look forward to a life of peace and contentment.
Look forward to a path of hope, not to a path of despair.
Never look back for the promise of tomorrow is to always look
forward.

MY SISTER SELMA

I have a sister
Whose character is as beautiful as her countenance.

I have a sister
Who has weathered tragedies that would have laid most people low.
She grew stronger with each tragic blow.

I have a sister
Who met every task head on.
No task too large. No task too small.
No task too menial. No task too great.

I have a sister
Who was a mother to all.

I have a sister
Who is an angel before her time.

I have a sister
Who makes one swell with pride.

I have a sister
Who is a blessing to all who know her.

I have a sister
That just to know her is to love her.

ODE TO THE YOUNG

Youth is a treasure.
Spend it well.

Use it, do not abuse it.

All too soon it will disappear
As fine sand between the fingers.

When it is gone, the soul will cry out:
"Alas! Where did it go?"

THE INNOCENCE OF TRUE BEAUTY

A baby so sweet and dear, you want to pick her up and hold
        her near.
Skin so smooth and clear with eyes so bright you felt as if a
        newborn saint was here.
Mother and child so bright and cheerful you knew that grand-
        mother was also near.
Pride in the creation of one so dear that grandmother and
        mother shed tears of delight.
This bundle of love radiated bountiful joy for all.
All who saw Baby Jacey Victoria knew that she was a treasure
        to behold.
Grandmother and mother swelled with pride at every glance at
        their bundle of joy.
The delicate beauty of her countenance reflects the beauty of
        her noble name, Jacey Victoria.
In the end it is true: "The apple does not fall far from the tree."

WELCOME THE BIRTH OF A NEW DAY

Awake each day with joy in your heart.
Each new day is a treasure.
Accept it as thus.
Accept the challenges of each new day, whether they are good
    or bad.
Remember each day is unique.
Each day is a golden day as it may be your last.
Treat it as a treasure close to your heart.
Recognize that all the years of each life is only a whisk of time in
    the annals of eternity.

A TRUE FRIEND

A true friend is one who knows you yet likes you.

A true friend is one who stands with you when things are grim.

A true friend is one who picks you up when you are on your knees.

A true friend befriends you when you stand alone.

A true friendship is a thing of beauty.

A true friendship stands at the zephyr of human relationships.

A true friend gives of oneself without thoughts of reward.

A true friend is a giver as well as a receiver in this most treasured human relationship.

Blessed are those who have a true friend.

A DAY WITHOUT PAIN

Tis a day when I hear the birds sing in all their glory.

Tis a day when I see the sun glisten on the morning dew as
nature's polished diamonds.

Tis a day the flowers bloom in all their brilliant colors.

Tis a day when my soul soars aloft on the wings of freedom.

Tis a day *Without Pain*.

TO MY BELOVED

I wrap you in the blanket of my love.
I take care of you with my devotion.

As I see my dear wife, my beloved, slip into the abyss of total
forgetfulness my heart aches for there is no cure for the
curse of this dreaded disease.

As we approach the deep gorge of the Rubicon, it is for all of
us to remember there is no return.

The fate of all is the same, the rich and the poor, the wealthy
and the destitute, the strong and the weak, the young and
the old. All are cursed with this dreadful plague.

It is for us who escape the ravages of this dreadful plague to
remember we are blessed. We must not keep this blessing
only for ourselves. We must spread the soothing balm of
our blessing for all who are ravaged by this curse of the
aging, especially to the dear ones whom we treasure
beyond words of expression.

Always remember: "That for the grace of God there go I."

OUR LOVE

To My Precious Wife

Our Love has bound our souls as one.

Our Love has joined our hearts beating as one.

Our Love is our shield, our gladiator, our protector from all that
stands in our way.

Our Love shall raise you up from your bed of thorns.

Our Love shall renew your life.

Our Love shall make our dreams come true.

Our Love shall make the joys and happiness of our
togetherness reborn.

Our Love shall be the aura of our lives.

Our love shall make this a reality.

ON MOTHER'S DAY TO MY DEAR WIFE

My eyes are the windows to my heart.

When you look into my eyes,
You will see my love for you
Pour through my veins with every throb of my heart.

Treasure this love, my dear,
For it is unique and everlasting.

Sweetheart, I love you on this Mother's Day
And for all the days of our lives and throughout eternity.

HOPE

As I lie here in the wee hours of the morning, my thoughts turn
to the days of yesteryear.

As the gentle breezes drift through the open window, I see
myself lying on the beautiful white sands of the beaches of
the mighty Pacific.

The gentle breezes wash over me with a delicate touch and
caress, cleansing my body and my spirit.

But, Alas!
Those days are gone forever.

But there is a bright future ahead.

On the distant horizon I glimpse the golden promise of
tomorrow and many tomorrows yet to come.

Once again I walk hand in hand with my friend, my sweetheart,
my wife to our golden future.

Once again I walk with a heart full of love for you, dear friend,
sweetheart, wife.

THE SPIRIT OF HOPE

Sweetheart, your life has been one of sorrow and tears.

Take solace in our years of togetherness and love.

Throw off the cloak of hopelessness.

It is for us to bring love, peace, and contentment as we bravely walk the paths ahead.

Let us treasure each passing day as if it is our last day.

The love we have for each other shall ease the burdens we carry.

We must remember the truth that love can conquer all.

Always with love and hope.

TO MY DEAR WIFE

The crucible of your sickness tests your mettle.
The agony of your pain tests our soul.

The depths of your despair yawns as an open pit.
The bowels of the earth quiver and groan in concert with your
    upheaval.

All is not lost.
Look up!

The faint rays of the sun shine through the clouds of hopelessness.
Throw off your cloak of despair.
Rid yourself of the demon of hopelessness.

A bright tomorrow looms before your very eyes.
It is more than hope.
It is a certainty!

I love you dearly.

TEARS OF SORROW

I weep tears of sorrow for my loving wife.
I weep the tears of sorrow for in the twilight of our lives, the love, the joys, and the happiness have been stealthily stolen away.
I weep the tears of sorrow for the springtime of our love and lives.
I weep the tears of sorrow for the meticulous wife of not so long ago.
I weep the tears of sorrow for the beautiful smile.
I weep the tears of sorrow for our many adventures, always together, have been taken away.
I weep the tears of sorrow for there is no answer to this human tragedy.
I weep the tears of sorrow in silence and alone for there is no one to care.
I weep the tears of sorrow for they shall cleanse my soul.
I weep the tears of sorrow for, in the end, they shall nurture the plant of life.

TEARS OF SADNESS

There are tears of joy and there are tears of sadness.

Tears of sadness fill my heart.

Tears of sadness well up in my eyes when I see my wife, my
love, withering away.

Tears of sadness cannot blot out the memories of joy and
happiness and love we have had for these many years.

Tears of sadness shall never be allowed to take you away in my
dreams and when I am awake.

Tears of sadness cannot take you away, for we are bound
together in life and throughout eternity.

A LIFE TIME

I weep for my love as I see her fade away before my eyes.

A lifetime of togetherness.

A lifetime of joy and happiness.

A lifetime with a veil of tears and sadness to dampen our joys and our happiness.

A lifetime filled with hope for love, for peace and for contentment in the closing days of our lives.

A lifetime of hope crashing on the unseen shoals of life.

A lifetime seeking the meaning of all that transpires before us.

A lifetime, no matter how brief, to resurrect our hopes, our dreams, our joys through the power of our love.

THE VEIL OF DESPAIR

When I sit with my beloved, the time clock of our lives spins
backwards.
It spins to the time in our lives when we met the challenge of
each new day, good or bad, with enthusiasm.
Today we are sealed in the tragedy of the affliction that has
enveloped my dear one.
The chain that binds us to a life of despair is stronger than that
of the finest steel.
We seek, by any means to rend asunder The Veil of Despair
that has shackled our lives.
But to no avail!
As we sink slowly into the morass of our bondage, the struggle
to escape only tightens the chains of our despair.
We must not, we cannot, allow ourselves to surrender to the
futility of our despair.
We must, at any cost, continue the struggle to find The Golden
Key which will unlock the chains of our bondage.
Escape into oblivion is not the answer!
We must realize that one day The Veil of Despair will dissipate
with the discovery of the Golden Key for our salvation.
With this discovery the bright, bright light of a new day shall
uplift our spirits and our souls.
As each new day dawns, our hope and our prayer is that this
will be the day that the great discovery of the Golden Key
shall be found.

THE SHIP OF LIFE

Our Ship of Life has crashed on the unmarked shoals of the Sea
    of Life.

We who navigate the Sea of Life have charted a course free of
    barriers, free of reefs, and other dangers of the sea.

But to no avail!

The Sea of Life has dangers that are unmarked, that are un-
    charted. With dangerous, jagged reefs just below the water
    line of a placid sea at rest.

These dangers rise and smite us when least expected!

No plan, no chart can guide us through the dangerous course
    we follow when we sail the Sea of Life.

The dangers that are part of sailing the Sea of Life are not
    anticipated, not planned for and thus we are struck a vital
    blow when we are unaware of the danger.

When our Ship of Life crashes an uncharted shoal or a jagged
    reef of the Sea of Life, we are cast adrift as lonely and
    desolate passengers without direction or control of our
    ultimate destiny.

We must! We have to once again grab the wheel that directs
    our passage on our Ship of Life.

We must chart a safe course to a distant land far off and beyond
    the horizon.

This will give us purpose!

This will give us hope!

This will light a safe course to our ultimate destiny.

DREAMS AND MEMORIES

Dreams of the night are the realities of day.
Dreams are a treasure that no one can steal away.
Dreams are the safe-keepers of our memories.

The jagged edges of our trials and tribulations of yesteryears
have been rounded into gentle curves that are polished by
the passage of time.
As simple drops of water wear away the mightiest and
everlasting mountains into gentle valleys and rolling hills, the
passage of time wears away the sharp edges of our distant
past into gentle polished memories.
These polished memories are stored for safe keeping in our
dreams.

Thus we reach back in to our dreams to the days of yesteryear
for the bright and glorious days of our life.
These memories are the solace for the travails of today.
Thus the trials and tribulations of the days of yesteryear fade
away.

The joys and happiness of those days, long gone, stand as a
beacon of light and hope shining on the memories and
dreams of those past days of glory.
As the days of yesteryear cannot be resurrected, the dreams
and memories of those days can be a fountain of hope to
sustain the lives of today.

Bask in the glorious days of yesteryear for they are the paths to
new hope and deeds of today.
With the sun high in the sky and the gentle breezes, the road
ahead is for more glorious days of living.

Dreams, memories and hope never die!

ON GROWING OLD

Is it our lot to wear the white mantle of our years?

Is it our lot to grow old with grace and dignity?

Is this to be the climax of our years?

Nay! We shall escape the prison of our years.

For we shall never grow old so long as we soar aloft on the
    dreams of youth.

THE GOLDEN YEARS

To grow old with grace and dignity is truly the Golden Years.
Blessed are those who enjoy the grace and dignity of these
twilight years.
Those who are robbed of this great moment of life through no
fault of their own, the Golden Years become the Stolen Years.
There is no joy or satisfaction in the lives of their loved ones when
they see and feel the pain of these Stolen Years.
Theirs is only one true course to follow. Those who love their
dear ones caught in this vicious trap must offer their dear ones
boundless love.
This love will make the giver of this love stronger and more
steadfast as they live out the days of their lives.
This love will make the giver of this love stronger and more
steadfast in their care and devotion to the ones who may not
consciously know that they are so deeply loved.
It is true: *Love can conquer all.*
Give this love without any expectation of return or reward. Give
this love to your dear ones and for oneself.
It is a blessing to be loved.
It is a greater blessing to give this love.
As flowers bloom in the brightness of the day, so shall the lives of
all bloom in the brightness of this love.

THE STOLEN YEARS

As the doctor utters the dreaded word, Alzheimers, fear grips
the hearts of the loved ones.
They know that there is no relief from this scourge of the
elderly.

The blessings of a longer life is a two-sided coin.
To those that escape the dramatic infirmities of their years, many
develop severe infirmities as they grow older.

The most debilitating, the most dreaded of these infirmities is
Alzheimers.
This scourge steals away the joys and promises of the Golden
Years.

The dream of a Golden Sunset at life's end grows dimmer with
each passing day.
The promise of the Golden Years fades away in to the reality of
the "Stolen Years".
The promise of a Golden Sunset at life's end becomes a
nightmare of sullen tumultuous storms with nary a bright light
seen through the clouds of despair.

The ravages of forgetfulness steal away the simple pleasures of
these later years.
The expectation of happiness in a long life of togetherness is
ripped asunder by this scourge of the elderly.
Thunderous clouds of despair obscure the beauty of the Golden
Sunset dreamt of in the final years of life.

In the terrible scheme of life, the scourge of the elderly effects
all.
None can escape the talons of Alzheimers if they fall victims of
this most dreaded scourge.

Neither the mighty nor the weak!
Neither the rich nor the poor!
Neither those in high places nor those in low places!

To those who escape the talons of this dreaded scourge,
    reward yourself by being the patient, the self-giving
    caregiver to those loved ones who have fallen victims of this
    dreaded disease.

Always remember that love is a powerful potion in curing all
    diseases of life.
Give this love willingly.
Give this love without expectation of any return.
Give this love to your life's soul-mate.

MORE IMPORTANTLY

Give this love for the goodness of your soul.
This love shall become the redeemer of the promised luster of
    the Golden Sunset so vicariously stolen away.

TWILIGHT

What a beautiful time of the day.

What a beautiful time of life.

As the faint light of the day dims, so do the cares of the day
fade away.

As the light of life begins to dim, so do the cares of life fade
away.

Embrace the soft light at day's end.

As we must, embrace the soft light at life's end.

As the soft light of the day fades away, the problems, the
turmoil of the day also fade away.

As the soft light of life fades away, we shall see the bright lights
of paradise ahead.

OH! WHERE DID THE YEARS GO?

Yesterday, I was twenty.
Today, I am eighty.
Oh! Where did the years go?

Yesterday, the children were small.
Today, the grandchildren are tall.
Oh! Where did the years go?

Yesterday, the dawn of new day was invigorating and challenging.
Today, we let each day slip by with barely a murmur.
Oh! Where did the years go?

Yesterday, I was tall, strong, and bronzed.
Today, I am bent over, weak, and gray.
Oh! Where did the years go?

Yesterday, each day was full of life, full of bustle, full of hustle.
Today, each day is dull and dreary, waiting patiently for each meal
     time.
Oh! Where did the years go?

Yesterday is gone forever!

Today is the day to throw off the cloak of despair.
Today is the day to let the light of each new day reveal the true
     glories of each and every day.
Today is the day we no longer cry out: Oh! Where did the years
     go?
Today is the day we know that the best years are yet to come!

ON MOURNING

Do not mourn when I am gone.

For the earth will spin on its axis.

For the earth will circle the sun.

For the stars shall sparkle in all their brilliance as before and
hence.

For I shall be wrapped in the cloak of eternity as I walk hand in
hand with God.

AN ODE TO THE CARDIAC REHAB ARTISTS

So adept, so unoppressive is the style of the Rehab Artists.
These Artists must be blessed by the divine.
It is commonly said: "That to be patient is to be divine."
Each and every one of these Artists has a special brand of
    divinity.

Old grouchy men are taken by the hand and are guided to a
    way of life left behind eons ago.
Elderly critical women are given the same treatment.

Each and every day of exposure to this patient and divine
    treatment restores and rejuvenates the very lives of those
    whose lives are still anchored in the bandage of yesteryears.
Once again they become the boys and girls of their long ago
    youth.

Their hearts and bodies have been reborn.
More importantly, their spirit, the excitement of a new life, has
    been reborn.
The rebirth of their bodies have allowed their spirits and souls to
    soar aloft by the hidden balm dispensed by these Artists of
    the Physique who have the golden touch.
Their reward is to witness the renaissance of those who
    believed that a full life was behind them.
The essence of their calling can be poignantly expressed by the
    ancient Hebrew philosopher and theologian of two
    thousand years ago, Hillel, who simply said: "If I am not for
    myself who will be? But, if I am only for myself what am I?
    If not now, when!"

Gifts from the heart are the most treasured of all.
You are all blessed.

DEMENTIA: THE CURSE OF THE AGED

A world of lost souls.

They wander aimlessly through the halls and corridors of their care-giving habitats, as good or as bad as they may be.

They seek a meaning to their lives as they sink slowly into the abyss of their affliction.

They are truly lost in the Time Warp of their existence. At times they are bright and witty.

At times they are sullen and withdrawn. At times they are completely catatonic. At times they are completely immobile. At times they are hyperactive. Where does it all end?

Do they continue to sink, ever so slowly into a life of oblivion?

Do they continue to function as human beings, with only the basic responses to the primary stimulus of life?

Yes! As they sink into a world of their own, they slowly lose all the basic stimulus of life.

In the end (some slowly and others rapidly), they return to the life of a fetus!

As such there is no response to the requisites of a living human being.

Thus their lives come to a timely end!

Let us all pray for the souls of those who are lost in the Time Warp of their lives.

A SALUTE TO THE CAREGIVERS OF THE AGED

In appreciation of the Caregivers who willingly give of
themselves to those who can no longer fend for themselves.
The Caregivers have the patience of the Saints.
The Caregivers have the soft touch of a mother.
The Caregivers have the wisdom of Job.
The Caregivers are angels who come in all colors and
nationalities.
The Caregivers willingly perform tasks from the most menial to
the near skills of a trained professional.
The Caregivers understand the infirmities of age whether these
infirmities are physical or mental or both.
The Caregivers are truly Angels without Wings.

OUT OF THE BLUE

Out of the Blue, a great city is brought to its knees; a great
nation is sorely bent, but not broken.

Out of the Blue, death rides the skyways of a magnificent
metropolis.

Out of the Blue, the cornerstone of a great nation's military
might, its nerve center, is laid low with a deafening roar of
death and destruction.

Out of the Blue, religious fanatics controlled the plans, the
dreams and the very lives of innocent mortals.

Out of the Blue, the standards of the good life, taken for
granted, were trashed against the melted, twisted steel and
slabs of concrete of two great symbols of a precious
heritage.

Out of the Blue, those who hate America filled their streets with
cheers and salutations. Crying out: "Allah Akabar," God is
Great, for what their kin had rendered. All the while, their
hypocritical leaders wept crocodile tears with words of
regret and condolence.

Out of the Blue, a great nation was shocked out of its smugness
and complacency.

Out of the Blue, the twisted steel, the slabs of concrete, the
death and destruction aroused the sleeping giant.

Out of the Blue, this great nation will restore, for itself and all
mankind, the sanctity and preciousness of life.

Out of the Blue, "The Right to Life, Liberty, and the Pursuit of
Happiness shall be resurrected in all its Beauty and
Grandeur.

THE BELLS OF SORROW

The Bells of Sorrow toll for those who perished on 9-11 and
for those they left behind.
The physical scars belie the depth of the emotional scars.
These scars are deep and everlasting.
These scars are not visible to the naked eye.

The evil doers have not been brought to bay since 9-11 and a
year and a day.
The weak and the strong still quiver on the mere thoughts of that
evil day.
Oh! Where is the power of the earth's mightiest that the evil
doer is preparing for another day of total death,
devastation, and destruction.

We hear mighty words of glorious triumphs. But where is the
prey?
Silence should be the order of the day.
The pelts of the evil doers should be hanging from the belts of
the brave soldiers of this mighty power.

Words and more words.
Is this the balm to ease our souls?
Is this the balm to uplift our spirits?
Is this the balm that will restore peace and tranquility throughout
our land?

Nay!
Only complete victory will be the balm that uplifts our souls.
Only complete victory will be the balm that uplifts our spirits.
Only complete victory will restore peace and tranquility
throughout our land.

The entire free world cries out for complete victory over the

forces of evil.
Words of glory!
Deeds of naught!
Shed the cloak of deceit.
Speak the truth and only the truth.

The true path for our great nation and the entire civilized free
    world is expressed in one word.
Victory!
Speak that word when victory is clearly in our grasp.
Then and only then will the Bells of Sorrow cease to toll.

DEAD OR ALIVE?

Wanted: Dead or Alive was the sheriff's slogan of the Old
    West for bandits of that era.
The town sheriff hung posters of the wanted bandits on the
    walls and poles in the towns in which the bandits operated.
The amount of the rewards for the captured bandits, dead or
    alive, were on these posters.
In those days there was no need for a trial of these wanted
    bandits. Either they were brought in dead or would soon be
    hanging.
No hassle, no trial. The verdict was always guilty as charged.
On the days that followed 9/11, the Great Sheriff of the United
    States issued from the White House a Dead or Alive
    manifesto for the most destructive bandit-terrorist, Osama
    bin Laden, in the history of America.
The pictures of this most notorious bandit-terrorist were posted
    throughout the world. All newspapers, magazines,
    television, and the Internet carried the likeness of bin Laden.
The reward for the capture of this essence of evil, dead or alive,
    was the astronomical sum of twenty-five million U.S. dollars
    ($25,000,000).
Tempting!
But now, more than four hundred and thirty days have passed
    since the most dastardly destructive deeds ever committed
    upon Americans on American soil with over three thousand
    dead and many thousands wounded, not one claimant has
    come forward to claim the reward.
This tells us something!
The Great Sheriff of the United States no longer cries out for
    the scalp of the bandit-terrorist, bin Laden.
The stillness emanating from the Great Sheriff's White House in
    regards to his eloquent Dead or Alive manifesto is
    deafening.
Now!

The Great Sheriff of the United States has laid out plans for new
worlds to conquer.

The Great Sheriff of the United States has stilled his bravado in

regards to the super bandit-terrorist, bin Laden, and has turned
his posse on to a fixed target.

The new bandit-terrorist is and has been a long time risk to the
Americans, as has Osama bin Laden. But this terrorist has a
fixed and permanent location, Iraq.

At long last, the Great Sheriff's posse knows where to look.
Iraq is on all the geographic maps of the world.

The new great bandit-terrorist, Sadam Hussein, has become the
new target of the Great Sheriff.

With a new target, the Great Sheriff hopes to divert his failures
in his quest for bin Laden to a much easier target, Saddam
Hussein.

Behold!

The mighty strength of the worlds only super power has failed in
its quest to capture or kill (Wanted: Dead or Alive) the
greatest enemy of America in modern times.

Shame! Shame!

The Great Sheriff of America shouts words of Glory to
aggrandize his stature.

Awake!

Awake America before it is too late!

Awake to the duplicity in the words of Glory and the deeds of
Naught.

America Beware!

As a brilliant political philosopher of the nineteenth century so
succinctly stated: "Patriotism is the last refuge of
scoundrels."

THE DEPTHS OF HATE

Hate devours the soul. Hate spreads its deadly venom and
    poisons whomever it touches.
The dogma of religious hatred is a venom that poisons the very
    lives of its adherents. The poisons of hate curdles the blood
    of all who consume this venom.
The poisons of hate instilled in the young is the springboard of
    the suicide bomber. These corrupted innocents willingly
    and gladly sacrifice their lives to satisfy their craving for the
    insidious poisonous potion of hate.
The venom of hate has brought a new form of warfare on the
    scarred and embattled civilization of humanity.

Beware!
No country, no society, no people are immune to the poisons of
    hate!
The venom of hate poisons the brain!
The venom of hate poisons the very fabric of humanity!
The venom of hate corrupts the love of the parent for the child.
They gladly place their offspring on the altar of hate to satisfy
    their craving for the insidious venomous potion of hate.

A life consumed by the poisonous addiction to the venom of
    hate is a life not worth living.
A society addicted to the insidious venom of hate is a society
    doomed to extinction.
The venom of hate is truly the Devil's Brew.
Those who indulge in this Devil's Brew shall live in hell before
    their time!

THE HOT WINDS OF HATE

The Hot Winds of Hate devour the very heart and soul of
civilization. The Hot Winds of Hate have spanned the entire
globe.

The Hot Winds of Hate have descended upon America from
the great valley of the Mississippi, to the mighty skyscrapers
of the Eastern Seaboard, to the very heart of our national
security.

The Hot Winds of Hate must be eradicated before the entire
earth becomes a wasteland of death and destruction.

The Hot Winds of Hate are stoked by the fires of those who
preach their brand of religion by extolling those who reap
death and destruction upon those who they deem to be
infidels. These preachers of hate praise those who are
willing to sacrifice their lives by killing babes in the arms of
their mothers.

The Hot Winds of Hate must be reduced to gentle breezes of
tolerance and understanding before all is lost.

The Hot Winds of Hate thrive on Man's Inhumanity to Man.
This is the spark that ignites the flames of hate.

Awake Humanity before it is too late!

Douse the flames of hate with the simple doctrine of Man's
Humanity to Man.

THE DISCIPLES OF THE DEVIL INCARNATE

The Disciples of the Devil Incarnate hold aloft the symbol that
    preaches hate and destruction and death of those who do
    not accept and believe in their conception of a religious
    faith.

All nonbelievers are infidels.
All infidels do not have the right to live.
All infidels must be eliminated for their lives have no meaning.
All infidels, from babes in the arms of their mothers, the young
    and the old, the innocent and the guilty, are the targets for
    death by the disciples of this perverted faith.

The blood of the nonbeliever on the hands of The Disciples of
    the Devil Incarnate is their key to paradise.
The hands of these disciples dripping with the blood of inno-
    cents, whom they have slain, are raised high as a token of
    their victory over the cursed infidel.
They raise their bloody hands high into the sky so all who
    believe as they do can salute their evil accomplishment.

Oh! Where is the true God of Compassion, of Justice, of
    Mercy and Forgiveness?
This God is not to be found in the minds of The Disciples of the
    Devil Incarnate.
The only goal of these perverted disciples is to reap death and
    destruction.
The God of Compassion, of Justice, of Mercy, of Forgiveness
    will doom those who desecrate His Commandment:
Thou Shall Not Kill.

These perverted disciples cast aside His Commandment.
They worship the false god who thwarts the Commandment:
Thou Shall Not Kill.

In the end, The Disciples of the Devil Incarnate shall suffer the
    same fate as the Ancients who defied God's Commandment.

All must come to the realization that there are many paths to the
    peak of the mountain.
All must have the right to choose their own path.
This simple, but bold concept will lead to religious peace and
    tolerance throughout the world.
With this worthy ideal in place, a far better world will emerge with
    universal recognition of all to have "The Right to Life, Liberty,
    and the Pursuit of Happiness."
This will become the beacon that will light the world!

BEGUILED—BEWITCHED—SUICIDAL

The young, the innocents willingly die before they taste the first fruits of life's maturity.

Those who lead these young innocents to an untimely death with the promise of eternal Paradise in the hereafter. All the while kept themselves safe and sound in their homes and hearth.

These preachers of Paradise in the hereafter treasure their lives. No suicidal destruction at the cost of their lives, the young, the beguiled, the bewitched are brain washed to put their heads on the cutting block for naught.

It is time to expose these monsters of hate for the Evil they induce in those who are mere babes in the world of hate created by their elders.

The very existence of these monsters who hide behind their distorted views of their religion where every nonbeliever is an infidel and is deserving of death and destruction. Rip off their veil of deceit and perversion and expose them for the evil they truly are.

Where are the true prophets who preach forgiveness, for understanding and the truth of "the sanctity of each and every life?" These prophecies are not found in the minds of those who hate!

All must remember that there are many paths to the summit of the lofty mountain of the hereafter. Each must have the right to choose their path to the summit of their own free will and choice.

To those who are beguiled, bewitched and suicidal throw off this cloak of deceit. Taste life's mature fruits to its fullest.

The hereafter is there for all eternity!

AN ODE TO A FIVE YEAR OLD

A monster in the disguise of a human invades a home.
A startled little girl looks up and sees this essence of evil.
The pure innocence of this tiny mortal is struck down with a
weapon of war not meant for the likes of her.
Oh where are the voices of civilization?
The silence of a prejudiced world is deafening.
A world that holds one people to a standard of restraint and
submission to terror as no other people.
A special place must be reserved in the hereafter for innocent
babes struck down by the cruelest of cruel enemies.
All the while these demoniac killers are hailed as heroes and
martyrs. These killers are evil incarnate. They shall pay the
price for their satanic endeavors.
Where do those who suffer the torture of their tragedies turn to
for solace and comfort?
Surely not to the standard of a society that holds these demons
to a level far below the level of their victims.
This evil with its attendant destruction of all life as a legitimate
weapon of their war.

The soul of humanity should cry out for justice!
The soul of humanity should cry out for compassion!
The soul of humanity should cry for the sanctity of all life!!

THE POOR JEW

The Jew is supposed to be the best Christian.
The Jew is supposed to walk the extra mile.
The Jew is supposed to "turn the other cheek."
The Jew is supposed to allow the guns of his enemies to mow
    him down.
The Jew is supposed to allow his enemies to burn his body to a
    crisp in the ovens of hatred.
The Jew is supposed to allow himself to be exterminated.
When the Jew is no more, his supposed-to-be friends will say:
    "Look what happened to the Poor Jew."
Never Again! Never Again! Never Again!

THE ALTAR OF GREED

Those who worship at the Altar of Greed have enshrined the Golden Calf.

Those who worship at the Altar of Greed bow down to this false idol.

Those who worship at the Altar of Greed care the least about the welfare of this Great Nation.

Those who worship at the Altar of Greed reap the most bountiful harvest.

Those who worship at the Altar of Greed are those who are at the helm of our Ship of State.

Those who worship at the Altar of Greed are responsible for the safety, the well being, the very lives of the citizens of this Great Republic.

Those who worship at the Altar of Greed have the power to manipulate the system for their sole benefit.

Those who worship at the Altar of Greed will lead all of us in to disaster.

Those who worship at the Altar of Greed take literally only a portion of the admonishment of Saint Paul who said in the scriptures: *To those that have more shall be given and to those who have not, that which they have shall be taken away.*

Those who are at the helm of our ship of State must disavow the false idol they have enshrined on the Altar of Greed.

Those who are at the helm of our Ship of State must return to the simple statement enunciated by our Founding Fathers who said: *All men are created equal.*

We live in dangerous times!

Let the captains of our Ship of State remember the words of wisdom of those who were willing to sacrifice their "lives, their fortunes, and their sacred honor," who said: "Either we hang together or we will hang separately."

THE MIGHTY HAVE FALLEN

The Giants of yesterday are the dwarfs of today.
The Nortels, the Enrons, the World Coms, the Global Cross-
 ings along with their bedfellows are pitiful supplicants at the
 bar of the Bankruptcy Courts.

The Mighty Have Fallen

Their hidden ill-gotten gains are no longer hidden.
The rape of their workers and the rape of their investors have
 strewn bloody financial carcasses across the economic
 landscape.
Who will rise in their stead?

Let those in high places remember that the brush of justice is
 broad.
Those who think that they can escape the wrath of the
 American people, let them be aware of the strength and the
 will to punish the evildoers.

Beware!
Do not attempt to hide behind the pillars of deceit.
The slightest breeze of honesty will topple these pillars of deceit.

There is no longer any place to hide for these evildoers.
The giants of the Nation must always remember "That what you
 are speaks so loudly that no one can hear you tell them
 what you are"!

In the End!
Honesty is the Best Policy

THE BOTTOM LINERS

Oh! Where is the love of America?
Oh! Where is the love of country that had made America great?
Oh! Where is the pride of this Nation that made America proud
     "From Sea to Shining Sea"?
Oh! Where is the great motto of America "E Pluribus Unum",
     out of many one?
This great motto of Americas is no longer to be found.

In its place those who wield the power in America have in-
     scribed the "Bottom Line" as the motto of this great Nation.
The new motto of America is "Unum", one (me). "May the
     devil take the hindmost".

The America of those who wield its power no longer value: "In
     God We Trust".
It has been replaced by the declaration: "In the Bottom Line We
     Trust".

The Bottom Liners flee their country looking for only one thing:
     Enhance the Bottom Line.
The road is clearly laid out for The Bottom Liners for they
     simply follow the path of starvation wages!

The hordes of the unemployed in nearby Mexico anxiously
     accepted any wage offered to them. Any wage is better
     than no wage at all
As the Mexican worker rose on the scale of subsistence, once
     again, The Bottom Liners sought out countries where huge
     masses of workers had no work of any kind.

The path was laid out pure and simple for The Bottom Liners.
They had no need to look any further than the huge masses of

unused workers of Asia who beckoned them with the siren
     song of starvation wages.
The Bottom Liners found their ultimate utopia in China's one
     billion, three hundred million people with legions of unem-
     ployed starving Chinese.
The masses of China's unemployed workers gladly accepted
     less than one-half the wages of the Mexican worker.

NOW!

The epitome of cost cutting through the media of starvation
     wages has started on industrial stampede to China.
The stampede of American industries controlled by The Bottom
     Liners is amazingly dramatic.
It is a Shot Across the Bow for America.

Awake America! Awake!
The workers of America, the backbone of this great Nation are
     "the lambs being led to slaughter" by The Bottom Liners.

The powers that be in the Capital of America are the willing
     partners to this great travesty.
The impoverishment at the workers of America lie at the
     doorstop of The Bottom Liners and their political cohorts.
The death of the Industrial Might of America is the result of the
     unholy alliance between The Greedy Bottom Liners and
     their governmental lackeys.
Step by step the mighty industries of America have been
     weaned away by impoverished workers of other countries
     where starvation wages are the opiate of The Bottom
     Liners.
The total dismantling of America's Industrial might is now
     clearly seen on the horizon!

The Rust Belts of America will spread with startling speed to all corners of the Nation.

The rust heaps of the once proud industrial might of America goes far beyond the factories.

The rust engulfs the workers, their families and the towns they live in.

These proud American workers are mortally stained by the industrial rust that spelled doom to many of America's finest industries.

Sadly, more fine American workers will be ordained for the same fate.

The Bottom Liners have achieved their goal. Costs are dramatically reduced and the Bottom Line has been dramatically increased.

The ultimate triumph of Greed!

Awake America! Awake!

Hopefully, there is a fatal flaw in the scheme of The Bottom Liners.

A poor America is not a consuming America.

Bottom Liners take heed for poor buyers are not good customers.

Bottom Liners you are on the path of the fable: You will kill "The Goose that laid the Golden Eggs".

It is true!

"As ye sow, so shall ye reap."

AN ODE TO A DYING PLANET

From the Blue Ice of the Arctic to the vast ice fields of
    Antarctica, what God has wrought, man has rend asunder.
From the mighty Andes to the lofty peaks of the Himalayas,
    what God has wrought, man has rend asunder.
From the rain forests of Brazil to the gigantic Redwoods of
    California, what God has wrought man has rend asunder.
From the Great Plains of America to the steps of Russia, what
    God has wrought man has rend asunder.
From the great sea of the Pacific to the smallest inlet, what God
    has wrought man has rend asunder.
From the surging Amazon to the Blue Danube, what God has
    wrought man has rend asunder.
From the lowest creature to the loftiest and mightiest creature,
    what God has wrought man has rend asunder.
From the Planet God has wrought let no Man further rend
    asunder.

DO UNTO OTHERS...

The Soul of Humanity cries out for compassion.

The Soul of Humanity cries out for justice.

The Soul of Humanity cries out for peace.

The Soul of Humanity cries out for an end to the Chants for War.

The Soul of Humanity cries out for the end to barbaric death and destruction.

The Soul of Humanity cries out for the protection of the weak, the poor, the young, the old, and the innocents.

Humanity can no longer survive under the Biblical Commandment of "An eye for an eye..."

The implementation of this commandment will doom Humanity to extinction.

The death of millions and more millions in a new conflagration will not solve the myriad problems confronting the Humanity of the World.

NAY!

The greater number of the dead; the maimed, the homeless shall only breed desire for greater destruction of lives and property.

Humanity must pay heed to the wise admonishment of the great Spanish philosopher, George Santayana, who simply stated: "Those who forget the lessons of history shall be doomed to repeat them."

The path to the Salvation of Humanity is clear and simple "Do unto others as you wish others do unto you!"

The Soul of Humanity must find the courage to take this bold but simple vital step.

DEATH STALKS THE INNOCENT

A Disciple of the Devil Incarnate stealthily breaches the security fence of a northern Israel Kibbutz.

In all the days of turmoil and death, this Israel farm community had been an oasis of peace and friendship.

The Israeli Jews and their nearby Arab neighbors had true friendly feelings, each for the other.

This oasis of peace was shattered by a Disciple of the Devil Incarnate.

The perverted Disciples take glory in the Death of the Innocent.

The mother of two toddlers coldly shot down at the door of her sons' bedroom.

Two toddlers, one four and one five, were coldly murdered as they cowered under the blanket of their bed.

God of Mercy what prevails on these perverted to shout to the world of their heroic act in the wanton slaying, in cold blood, of a pitiful mother and her two pitiful children.

Has the world gone mad when the wanton Death of the Innocent are proclaimed as heroic acts of bravery by the Disciples of the Devil Incarnate?

Oh!

Where is the cry of all humanity condemning this dastardly deed? The silence of the world is deafening!

All must realize that every act of evil has a price.

Blood begets Blood!

Beware!

The price of this dastardly deed will be oceans of blood of the perpetrators for their devilish acts and their victims alike.

All must come to the realization that the momentary victories achieved from the Death of the Innocent will come back to haunt the pseudo bravery of the Disciples of the Devil Incarnate.

Blood begets Blood!

There is only one true course to follow.

All must come to the realization that every life is precious.

All must come to the realization that all lives are lived on a two way street.

All must come to the realization of the truth of the statement: "Whom the gods will destroy they first make mad!"

All must come to the realization that it is true: "As ye sow, so shall ye reap."